P9-CCF-148

The Library
of Tattoos
and Body
Piercings

Tattoos, Body Piercings, and Art

By Kris Hirschmann

ReferencePoint
Press®

San Diego, CA

© 2014 ReferencePoint Press, Inc.
Printed in the United States

For more information, contact:
ReferencePoint Press, Inc.
PO Box 27779
San Diego, CA 92198
www.ReferencePointPress.com

ALL RIGHTS RESERVED.
No part of this work covered by the copyright hereon may be reproduced or used in any form or by any means—graphic, electronic, or mechanical, including photocopying, recording, taping, web distribution, or information storage retrieval systems—without the written permission of the publisher.

LIBRARY OF CONGRESS CATALOGING-IN-PUBLICATION DATA

Hirschmann, Kris, 1967-
  Tattoos, body piercings, and art / by Kris Hirschmann.
    pages cm. -- (The library of tattoos and body piercings series)
  Includes bibliographical references and index.
  ISBN-13: 978-1-60152-562-8 (hardback)
  ISBN-10: 1-60152-562-1 (hardback)
1. Tattooing--Juvenile literature. 2. Body piercing--Juvenile literature. 3. Body art--Juvenile literature. I. Title.
  GT2345.H57 2014
  391.6'5--dc23
                                                        2013005828

Contents

Are Tattoos and Body Piercings Art?

In an article titled "Are Tattoos Art?," author Nicolas Michaud presents a thought-provoking scenario: "Imagine that you're sitting on a bar stool in your favorite bar . . . when a large, angry-looking man walks in. The first thing you notice about him is the fact that his arms and neck are covered with tattoos. He sits down on the bar stool next to you, leather squeaking. You glance over, nervously, and say, 'Nice tattoo.' Smiling, your new friend replies, 'Thanks! It's a da Vinci.'"[1]

Michaud admits that this seems like an improbable turn of events. But, he points out, "a tattoo is an image presented to us on a surface and a Leonardo da Vinci painting is an image presented to us on a surface. What makes a tattoo all that different, then? . . . Is there any reason that we should not consider artistically crafted tattoos 'art' just as we would an artistically crafted painting art?"[2]

The question Michaud poses has been much debated in recent decades as the practices of tattooing and other types of body modification, including piercing, have risen dramatically in popularity. Skilled artists have flocked to these fields to fulfill the public demand. As a result of this talented influx, the quality of today's bodywork has skyrocketed. Many people feel that these practices have, indeed, achieved the status of fine art.

Did You Know?

Tattooing and body piercing fall under the larger category of "body modification." Body modification includes any deliberate alteration of the human body for nonmedical reasons.

A Boston tattoo convention provides a venue for body art aficionados to display their work. Tattoos and body piercings make up the world's oldest—and newest—fine art.

Tattoo and Piercing Basics

This particular art is created on human canvases. A tattoo is a permanent image within the skin. It is made by using needles or other implements to push ink into the dermis, which is the skin's bottom layer. The cells of the dermis are stable and do not change much over time. The ink therefore stays more or less where it is placed throughout the wearer's lifetime.

Body piercing is the practice of puncturing or cutting the human body to create an opening, usually meant to hold jewelry. On its own, a single small piercing does not have much artistic value. Many carefully arranged piercings, however, can create a striking effect. Elaborate jewelry can also add drama to a piercing display.

Although tattooing and body piercing have enjoyed a revival in recent decades, they are not new practices. These techniques have existed for thousands of years in cultures all over the world. They have been used for many purposes, including identification, religious marking, spiritual protection, and more. Of course, they have also been used simply to beautify the wearer. Many people through the ages have considered tattoos and body piercing to be personal and lovely works of art.

Did You Know?

A 2012 survey found that 21 percent of American adults have at least one tattoo. Only 7 percent have non-earlobe piercings.

Three Sides of the Debate

Views on this subject differ today. Some people vehemently reject the idea that body modification has any artistic value. "In my opinion, getting a tattoo is a foolproof way for a guy to look like a tool and a girl to look like a tramp,"[3] complains one writer. Other people object for religious reasons, pointing out that one biblical passage forbids cutting into the flesh or marking the skin. They feel that this prohibition is reason enough to look down on tattoos and piercings.

Still other people take a "maybe, maybe not" approach to the question. They think that really good, artistically rendered tattoos and piercings may qualify as art. Poorly executed work, on the other hand, does not make the grade. Michaud elaborates on this view: "A tattoo that can draw us in and move us deeply is one that would be considered art. On the other hand, a generic butterfly on the ankle would not be considered art—it would simply be a picture on a person,"[4] he says.

That last phrase, though—"a picture on a person"—may be the key that unlocks the answer. Generic ankle butterflies or simple nose rings may be deeply meaningful to the people who wear them. Michaud makes this point about tattoos, although it applies equally to piercings and other forms of body modification. "The fact that a tattoo is placed on a person adds a significant layer of context and potential meaning that makes tattoos a fertile ground for aesthetic experience,"[5] he says.

All this debate makes interesting food for thought, but it is a bit too academic for tattooing and piercing enthusiasts. These people feel strongly that artistic value is in the eye of the beholder—and from their perspective, body modifications look very good indeed. They are proud to be on the cutting edge of the world's oldest—and newest—fine art.

The Traditional Art of Tattoo

In the late 1600s an English expedition stumbled upon a remote island populated by fantastically decorated tribesmen. An expedition member later described one native with these words: "His whole Body (except Face, Hands and Feet) is curiously and most exquisitely Painted or Stained full of Variety and Invention with prodigious Art and Skill perform'd. . . . The Paint itself is so durable, which nothing can wash it off or deface ye beauty of it."[6]

The writer of this passage was describing a full-body tattoo. Such decorations were unknown in Europe and must have seemed incredibly exotic to the surprised Englishman. In other parts of the world, though, tattooing was a common practice. Men and women alike were expected to sport permanent markings on their bodies.

The extent of this decoration varied from culture to culture. Most groups favored small tattoos that were widely scattered on the skin. In a few regions, however, extensive and skillful tattooing was the norm. The cultures of the Pacific Islands and Japan, in particular, elevated the simple tattoo to an art form. The traditions born in these regions inspired much of the tattoo art that people still enjoy today.

Tattoos of Polynesia

A region called Polynesia is especially renowned for its tattoo artistry. Polynesia is a vast area that covers much of the central and southern Pacific Ocean. Roughly triangular, the region includes more than one thousand islands. Many of these islands have been home to thriving cultures for thousands of years.

Although marked differences are found among these cultures, there are many similarities as well. One of these similarities is a love of tattoo. Historians do not know how early this tradition developed. It is certain, however, that the art of Polynesian tattoo was well developed by the time European explorers started to arrive in the late 1500s. The natives' curious body art was mentioned as early as 1595 by a Spanish adventurer named Álvaro de Mendaña y Neira. The custom was further noted by later explorers, including the English captain Samuel Wallis, who wrote after a 1767 trip to Tahiti that it was a "universal custom among men and women to get their buttocks and the back of their thighs painted with thin black lines representing different figures."[7]

A few years later Captain James Cook of Britain's Royal Navy penned a similar report. "Both sexes paint their Bodys, Tattow, as it is called

A Polynesian tattoo artist, well-known for the quality of his traditional designs, shows off his own tattoos. The art of tattoo has been practiced in Polynesia for centuries.

in their Language,"[8] Cook wrote after a visit to one Polynesian island. This passage is the first known reference to the word spelled today as *tattoo*.

As time went by, it became obvious to European adventurers that the art of tattoo was widespread in Polynesia. Explorers of this region found stunning examples of body art practically everywhere they landed. They eventually learned that this art could have many meanings. It could reflect a person's age, wealth, strength, or power. It might have links to a person's job or personality—and it definitely communicated a person's status. More tattoos equaled more respect in the Polynesian culture.

Whatever their specific meanings, all of these tattoos had something in common: They were seen as beautiful, not just functional. Polynesian tattooists trained at length before they could practice their trade, and they took great pride in their artistic abilities and interpretations. From culture to culture and tradition to tradition, these artists were careful to make their human canvases as beautiful as their skills allowed.

Did You Know?

In the mid-1800s Christian missionaries decided Tahitian tattoos were signs of sin. They sometimes skinned tattooed natives to "cure" them of this malady.

A Trip to Tahiti

This was certainly the case in Tahiti, where both men and women bore elaborate, striking tattoos. A naturalist named Joseph Banks penned the earliest known description of these marks: "Every one is marked thus in different parts of his body. . . . Some have ill designed figures of men, birds or dogs, but they more generaly have this figure Z either simply, as the women are generaly marked with it, on every joint of their fingers and toes and often round the outside of their feet, or in different figures of it as square, circles, crescents &c. which both sexes have on their arms and legs; in short they have an infinite diversity of figures."[9]

The tattoos described in this passage varied from person to person in their design and arrangement. Banks noted, however, one important point of consistency among virtually all of the islanders. Their buttocks were tattooed a deep, uniform black, and their lower backs were crisscrossed with a series of elaborate arches. "These arches are their great pride: both men and women shew them with great pleasure, whether as a beauty or a proof of their perseverance and resolution in bearing pain I can not tell,"[10] Banks wrote.

The answer is probably a little bit of both. The tattooing process was long and painful, and enduring it definitely required great courage. Heavily tattooed skin was therefore seen as a proud display of bravery.

There is little doubt, though, that Tahitian tattoos were considered beautiful as well as symbolic. The region's tattoo artists took obvious

Dying for Their Art

The elaborate facial tattoos of the Maori fascinated early explorers. They wanted to share this unique artwork with their European countrymen back home. Lacking cameras, however, they could not simply take snapshots—so they brought the originals instead. From the late 1700s until the mid-1800s, preserved Maori heads were in great demand on the international art market.

This demand spawned a particularly bloody period in Maori history. Hungry for European money and goods, Maori tribesmen started killing each other to obtain tattooed heads. When they ran out of already tattooed neighbors, they began tattooing slaves' faces with traditional *moko* markings instead. As soon as the skin healed, the unfortunate slaves were beheaded and promptly traded in for cold, hard cash.

By the height of the head trade in 1830, this practice had become so prevalent that, explains one writer, "no man who was well tattooed was safe for an hour unless he was a great chief, for he might be at any time watched until he was off his guard and then knocked down and killed, and his head sold to the traders." This intolerable situation led to laws that made head trafficking illegal. The Maori head trade soon died down—but museums and private collections around the world still display the artifacts obtained during this gruesome period.

Katherine L. Krcmarik, "Tattooing in Tribal Cultures." Tattooing Around the World, Michigan State University, 2003. www.msu.edu.

pride in their work and rendered it as skillfully as possible. The artists' subjects, in return, were delighted with their permanently painted skin. They welcomed the pain that made them attractive in their society's eyes.

Marks of the Marquesas

Even more extreme were the tattoos of the Marquesas Islands. Lying about 850 miles northeast of Tahiti, the Marquesas had a booming tribal population during the time of the first European explorations. During this era tattooing was essential to the art, lifestyle, and personal identities of the islands' residents.

The tattooing process was more elaborate for Marquesan men than women. A boy got his first tattoos when he reached adulthood. The process was performed by a tattoo artist called a *tuhuna pati tiki*, which translates as "one who strikes or marks designs." The *tuhuna* and his assistants surrounded the tattoo subject and used a variety of sharp tools to pound a sooty paste into the skin. As they worked, they chanted encouraging verses to soothe their agonized human canvas. One verse reminded the subject how good he would look with his new tattoos:

We tap, yes we tap you a little, yes?
Who knows who will come look at the ta-tu of this fellow?
A Beautiful maiden will come, yes!
To look at the ta-tu of this fellow, who knows?[11]

Marquesan men evidently took such words to heart, because they seldom stopped at just one tattoo. Warriors in particular added new design elements to mark each battle victory or accomplishment. They tattooed every available body part, including the eyelids, the insides of the nostrils, the earlobes, and even the tongue and gums. During a warrior's lifetime, says one writer, "a man's epidermis was covered with layer after layer . . . until his body was black with designs."[12]

This artwork was highly individual and even sacred—so much so, in fact, that it was not allowed to outlast its owner. When a tattooed Marquesan man died, tradition demanded that his skin be removed before he could enter the afterlife. The man's female relatives had to rub the corpse with rough rocks to remove every scrap of decoration. Only when this task was complete could the warrior, his skin now returned to its birth state, be laid to rest.

Patterned Skin in Samoa

This extreme requirement was not part of the Samoan tattoo culture. The body art given to the young men of this Polynesian region was meant to follow its owners into the afterlife. A traditional Samoan tattooist's chant makes this fact clear:

> The necklace may break, the string may break
> But your tattoo will not break.
> This necklace of yours is permanent.
> And will go into the grave with you.[13]

Apart from this key difference, though, the tattoo traditions of Samoa were similar to those of the Marquesas. Young Samoan men from important families submitted to the needles of a tattoo artist called a *tufuga ta tau* around the age of fourteen. The process was highly ceremonial and symbolic, and it could last several months. When it was done, the subject was transformed. His skin bore bold, thick patterns from the midsection all the way down the buttocks and thighs. Even the scrotum was a canvas for this painful painting.

Such Samoan "leggings" are distinguished by several unique features. The overall design is divided into zones, such as the back, buttocks, and legs. Each of these zones has its own artistic motif. Themes are mostly drawn from nature and may include stylized insects, shells, and birds. A bat called the flying fox, or *pe'a*, is especially important in Samoan tattoo art. Symbolizing protection, the *pe'a* was thought to act as a built-in shield for those who bore its image.

Protection, of course, was not the only goal of traditional Samoan tattoos. As in other Polynesian tattoo cultures, artistic value was an important factor as well. The best Samoan tattoo artists were renowned for the careful symmetry of their designs and the fine compositions they created for their clients. The Samoan word *ta tau*, which translates to "correct or artfully done," echoes this sentiment. Both lovely and functional, the tattoos of this region were unquestionably the work of master artists.

Did You Know?

To administer a proper Marquesan tattoo took up to four months. The procedure caused swelling and fever and was sometimes fatal.

Moko of the Maori

The same was true of the elaborate facial tattoos of the Maori, the indigenous people of New Zealand. Worn by men, these pieces were known as *moko*. Each *moko* was crafted by a trained artisan called a *tohunga ta moko* and consisted of a one-of-a-kind combination of lines, swirls, and dots. The combinations were so unique that they acted as a sort of fingerprint. A Maori could be unerringly identified by the pattern etched into his face.

In 1769 Cook was one of the first Westerners to describe these patterns. "The marks in general are spirals drawn with great nicety and even elegance. One side corresponds with the other," he wrote. In the same source, the explorer went on to catalog body tattoos of a similar nature. "The marks on the body resemble foliage in old chased ornaments, convolutions of filigree work. . . . No two were formed alike on close examination,"[14] he noted.

The artistry of these fine lines and swirls became even more remarkable upon closer examination. The technique used by Maori tattoo artists involved chiseling ink into the skin with a blade called a *uhi* rather than injecting or poking it. The process was more traumatic than regular tattooing, and it left grooved scars on the subject's skin along with tattooed images. These scars, as well as the ink they carried, were a source of great pride for their owners. A well-tattooed man was considered not only attractive but brave, strong, and prestigious as well.

Maori women, too, used tattoo art to beautify themselves. They were not permitted to wear full *moko*, but they were allowed to tattoo their chins and upper lips. The pink flesh of the lips themselves was also a common site for tattoo work. The Maori inserted soot and other inks into the skin to improve upon what they considered the ugly red shade that nature had chosen for the human mouth.

Fine Art on Skin

Improving upon nature was also a goal in ancient Japan, another culture with a strong tattooing tradition. Tattooing, or *irezumi,* has been practiced in this area,

Did You Know?

In Samoa and the Marquesas Islands, tattooing was done in huts built especially for the occasion. The huts were destroyed when the tattoo work was complete.

The indigenous Maori people of New Zealand are famous for elaborate facial tattoos consisting of lines, swirls, and dots. This sculpted mask, displayed in a New Zealand museum, shows the traditional Maori tattoos.

it is believed, for over ten thousand years. The earliest Japanese tattoos were simple line patterns that had spiritual meaning, decorative purposes, or both.

The nature of Japanese tattoos changed over time. First, they moved from being simple decorations to status symbols for wealthy and important people. Next, they found a use in Japan's law enforcement system.

Convicted criminals were tattooed on their foreheads or forearms as a permanent warning to law-abiding citizens.

This criminal link squashed tattoos' popularity for quite some time. Around the year 1600, though, tattoos began to creep back into common use. Religious men had prayers tattooed on their backs. The members of some lower-class professions got matching tattoos to express support for their fellow workers. Loving couples got coordinating images on their hands, arms, and thighs to symbolize their eternal union. Slowly but surely, the art of tattoo became socially acceptable once again.

Outlaw Art

The art of Japanese full-body tattoo is famous around the world. In Japan itself, though, this practice is often regarded with suspicion. This is the case because full-body tattoos were once worn mostly by career criminals called *yakuza*. The *yakuza* were brutal and ruthless. Their tattooed skin intimidated enemies because it proved the owners were tough and could withstand intense pain.

Thanks to the *yakuza*, the link between tattoos and crime became firmly established in the Japanese mind. More than a century ago, this association was so strong that tattooing became illegal in Japan. The practice was legalized again in 1948. Until recently, though, getting a tattoo has still been considered unthinkable by most law-abiding citizens. As one historian says, "To be tattooed in Japan is to abandon conventional society and go into the underworld."

The general distrust of tattoos has relaxed in recent decades. Small designs in Western styles are now popular and accepted among Japanese youth. Full-body designs, however, still raise eyebrows. As a result, even modern *yakuza* are abandoning this fashion. In the modern world, it seems that even the most notorious criminals would rather be anonymous than feared.

Mieko Yamada, "Japanese Tattooing from the Past to the Present," Tattoos.Com Ezine, 2000. http://tattoos.com.

Tattoos might have been socially acceptable, but they had not yet reached artistically impressive heights. In the early 1800s, however, something happened that catapulted Japanese tattoo into an art form renowned around the world. The change occurred after a novel called the *Suikoden* was published. The novel concerns the adventures of legendary heroes, and it is lavishly illustrated with colorful woodcut prints. These prints excited and inspired people. They spawned an immediate demand for tattoos based on the novel's images.

In response, woodblock artists began tattooing. Using traditional woodworking tools such as hammers and chisels, they carved *Suikoden* images into people's flesh. The tools were big—and so were the finished designs. Covering the subject's entire back or even more flesh, these tattoos were the beginning of Japan's full-body tattoo tradition.

Did You Know?

The classic 1827 edition of the Japanese work titled *Suikoden* features woodcut prints of 108 heroes. These heroes are popular tattoo motifs to the present day.

A Grand Tradition

The art of woodcut-inspired *irezumi* quickly expanded from its humble origins. It was adopted by artists who abandoned woodcutting techniques and figured out ways to work exclusively with human skin. These artists developed special tools such as needle-tipped bamboo sticks. The needles were dipped in sooty oil, then inserted into the subject's skin. By performing this action over and over, the tattoo artist slowly created an image.

Using this method and others, Japanese tattooists grew more and more ambitious in their work. *Irezumi* spread from the back to the shoulders, arms, thighs, and eventually to the entire body. Artists were free to be creative in their work's arrangement and application. One popular design, for instance, covered the entire upper torso except for a vertical strip running from the chest to the abdomen. This unadorned strip made the tattoo look like it was hanging open, much like an unbuttoned vest.

While the patterns of the tattoos varied, the general style usually did not. Classic *irezumi* work echoed its woodcut origins with characteristic colors, motifs, and artistic approaches. It built upon these basics by tailoring them to fit each unique human canvas. The finished work, explains one author, ideally "[follows] the lines of the body, with particular attention to muscular movements. When the tattooed person moves his muscles the pictures come alive."[15]

This is not the only goal of *irezumi*. In a 2010 article the renowned Japanese tattoo artist Horihide explains that proper tattoos follow many traditional and sometimes obscure rules. For instance, he says, "There are four seasons (spring, summer, fall and winter) in Japan. The seasons should be expressed in tattoo art as well. . . . The untrained tattooists draw a snake and cherry blossoms, but this is a wrong way in tradition. When cherry trees begin to bloom in March in Japan, the snake still hibernates under the ground. . . . In other words, it does not make any sense if the snake and cherry blossoms are drawn together."[16]

Guidelines such as this one are not widely known. They tend to be passed down by word of mouth from teacher to student. For this reason

A respected Japanese tattoo artist creates elaborate and colorful tattoos using imagery from traditional Japanese culture. It takes decades of study and practice to achieve this level of artistry.

trained tattooists can easily spot mistakes made by less educated artists. It takes years or even decades of study and dedication to master the world's most complex form of tattoo.

Art Everywhere

The cultures of Polynesia and Japan may reign supreme when it comes to tattoo artistry. The people of these regions are not, however, the only ones who find tattoos beautiful. Decorative body art has a long history in many places, including North Africa, where the women of many Berber groups sport elaborate designs on their faces, hands, and feet. Tattoo is important in India's Kutch district, where women carefully apply traditional patterns to their arms and legs. And beautiful tattoos are considered a necessity in the Indonesian archipelago of Mentawai, where people decorate their skin to please their immortal spirits. As one author explains, "A person's soul would not feel at home in a body that was not artistically 'completed' with fine drawings."[17]

This comment points out something important about the tattoo mentality everywhere, not just in Mentawai. Many people love being living works of art. They feel like beautiful tattoos improve their outer and inner selves in many ways. Given this feeling, tattoo has, not surprisingly, risen to an art form in cultures around the world.

Did You Know?

In the 1800s the Japanese government forced many people to wear drab clothing. Historians think this law helped to launch Japan's tattoo tradition. People could not wear bright garments, so they decorated their skin instead.

Living Works of Art

Defense attorney Mary Lynn Price is middle-aged and clean-cut, and she works in an appearance-conscious profession. She might seem like an unlikely candidate for a tattoo. When surgery left a large scar across Price's belly, though, she made a bold decision: She decided to cover the damage with a tattoo. In an interview, Price describes her delight with the result. "There's no scar visible. . . . Now when I look at my body . . . I see something that's very beautiful and very magic."[18]

Price's experience has led her to ponder the deeper meaning behind tattoos. The answer, she believes, boils down to an urge—sometimes even a need—to stamp artwork permanently onto the body. "[People] ask, 'Well, why did you get a tattoo,' and then we'll give reasons. I think reasons tend to be the more superficial explanation, after the fact. There's something deeper going on. There's something far more profound and primal, and deeper to the motivation, to have one's skin, one's body [become] an artistic canvas,"[19] she says.

Price's insight may not apply to every tattoo enthusiast—but then again, it may. Many people appreciate tattoos for their artistic value, and some people take the concept a step further. They become fascinated or even obsessed with the process of decorating their skin. Over time, they come to think of themselves as living works of art.

Types of Tattoo Art

This transformation can take many forms. Tattoos can range from small, isolated images to full-body masterpieces. Although there are no hard-and-fast rules, many people who appreciate tattoos for their artistic value opt for larger designs.

The lower-back tattoo is one popular choice of this type. These tattoos span the small of the back. They are usually symmetrical, spreading out fairly evenly on both sides of the spine. Peeking out of the gap between low-cut jeans and cropped shirts, these pieces add an artistic touch to a sensual part of the human body.

Also popular is the sleeve or half-sleeve tattoo. As the name suggests, these tattoos cover part or all of the arm, just as a shirt sleeve would. Well-designed sleeves have themes that unify their many parts and say something about the wearer. Executed properly, they can be true works of art.

For extremists, the body suit or full-body tattoo may be irresistible. Body suits are tattoos that cover all or virtually all of the body, although the face, neck, and hands often remain bare. Like all tattoos, body suits can be done haphazardly, but the most striking examples have a pattern or theme that unifies the entire presentation. Achieving this look can be a challenge. One tattoo expert offers this sensible advice to people considering full-body work: "If you're going with a theme, try to use the same tattoo artist throughout the piece. Since each artist has their own unique style, if you truly want the entire piece to look exactly the same, you will have better luck if you use the same person."[20]

The tattoo process is time-consuming and expensive. It is also painful, especially in sensitive or thin-skinned areas. But many people consider the time, money, and pain well worth the result. They are willing to endure whatever it takes to turn their bodies into living canvases.

Most Tattooed Man

This is certainly the case for Lucky Diamond Rich, an Australian man who has held the Guinness world record for being the world's most tattooed man since 2006. Every scrap of Rich's skin has been tattooed, sometimes several times. Rich estimates that if he added up the surface area of all his tattoos, including the ones that have been tattooed over, his coverage would be about 350 percent. In other words, he has been completely tattooed three and a half times.

He has no intention of stopping, either. Rich freely admits that he is obsessed with the idea of ink on skin. He likes the process of being tattooed, and he likes

Did You Know?
Tattoo artists sometimes call neck and face tattoos "job blockers" because they cannot be hidden during job interviews, and many employers dislike them.

associating with the interesting artists who practice this trade. "I just really want to get tattooed by [him]," Rich enthused about one particular person in a recent interview. "I'm attracted to the characters of the tattoo world."[21]

Rich likes not just the tattoo process; he also loves the way his decorated skin looks. In an artistic sense, his interests range far and wide. "I'm into everything," he laughs. "My first body suit was a mixture of Japanese, old school, tribal, Viking. . . . Then I stepped into a whole new world—the white on black, black on black. . . . This is my way of sealing my place in the tattoo world!"[22]

In that he has succeeded. As one of the tattoo community's best-known members, Rich is in constant demand for personal appearances and interviews. People are hungry to see the world's most tattooed man in the flesh—and Rich revels in the attention. He never feels self-conscious because, he says, "[my body art] made me the person I am today, and that person is someone that is probably the most free spiritually because I'm in a place where I'm absolutely 100 percent comfortable with myself."[23] Rich knows he is a work of art, and he is happiest when he puts that art on display.

Peeling Away the Skin

Rick Genest, also known as "Zombie Boy" or "Rico the Zombie," is comfortable being on display, too. Genest, who is a native of Montreal, Canada, decided at age sixteen that his greatest ambition was to become a zombie. He could not achieve this goal in a genuine horror-movie sense, so he decided to reach it through the art of tattoo instead. Within a few years Genest had covered about 80 percent of his skin with tattoos of internal organs, bones, and peeling flesh. "They're about the human body as a decomposing corpse—the art of a rotting cadaver," he explains. "I see my tattoos as celebrating the art of obscenity and the macabre."[24]

The world has responded with enthusiasm to Genest's vision. Zombie Boy rocketed into the public view in 2011, when he was plucked from obscu-

Did You Know?

It is possible to tattoo the human eyeball. The process is dangerous and sometimes leads to blindness, but it is becoming popular anyway.

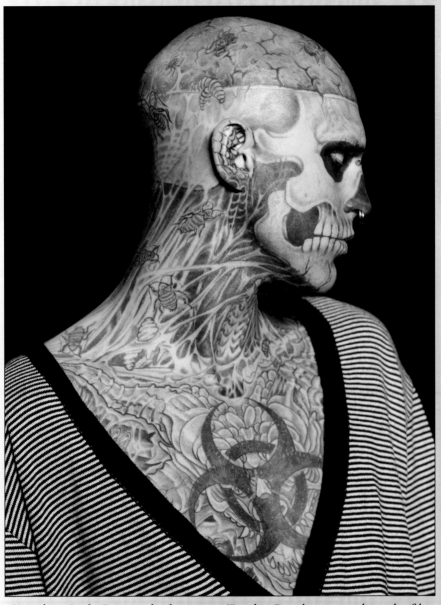

Canadian Rick Genest, also known as Zombie Boy, has covered much of his body with tattoos of internal organs, bones, and peeling flesh. His unusual body art has landed him various public appearances, including a spot in a Lady Gaga video.

rity to appear in Lady Gaga's video for the song "Born This Way." Soon afterward Genest landed a job as a runway model for several high-fashion clothing lines. He also appeared in a 2012 TV commercial for a concealing makeup called Dermablend, by L'Oreal. The ad shows an apparently unblemished Genest wiping off his makeup to reveal the rotting horror underneath. The underlying message? If this product can cover *that*, it can certainly take care of everyday wrinkles and spots.

Zombie Boy's newfound notoriety might seem to be at odds with his urge for individuality. When asked how he feels about his current popularity, though, Genest just shrugs. "I respect the industry," he says. "I've always surrounded myself with artists. I've always loved being around

Addicted to Tattoos

People often tell their friends that tattoos are addictive and that one usually leads to more—sometimes many, many more. Can the urge to be tattooed become a true addiction? A recent article examines the issue.

> As a general rule, an addiction is described as something that someone relies on, either physically or psychologically, and sometimes both. . . . When someone becomes addicted to something, he or she can engage in behavior that is harmful in pursuit of the experience or chemical required to satisfy physical or emotional needs. Addicts have difficulty prioritizing their life choices, opting for another hit of an addictive substance rather than the payment of a utility bill, for example. They persist with their behavior despite the physical, economic, and social consequences. . . .
>
> In order for someone to be considered addicted to tattoos, he or she would have to become physically or emotionally dependent on the process. In some cases, this may happen. . . . If someone chooses to get a new [tattoo] rather than coping with a situation, or pays for a tattoo before securing the rent, he or she may be addicted.

S.E. Smith, "Can I Really Get Addicted to Tattoos?," Wisegeek, November 29, 2012. www.wisegeek.org.

the art scene and the fashion world and designing sets and props and all of that. That's all showmanship, that's all art."[25]

It is—and for now, Genest is part of the scene. But Zombie Boy knows his situation could change at any time, and he is fine with that idea. All he really wants is to live his art. Through tattoo, he has already made that dream come true.

It's a Living

Zombie Boy did not expect his tattoos to make him rich or famous. His success was a happy accident. Other people, however, do see tattooing as a path to prosperity. They turn themselves into living pieces of art not because it is their passion but simply to make a living.

Tom Leppard chose this extreme path. After quitting his job and moving to a remote Scottish island, Leppard realized that he needed more cash to survive. He decided to tattoo his entire body with leopard spots to attract attention and, he hoped, a meager income.

The gamble paid off. Leppard's efforts were recognized by the *Guinness Book of World Records*. He also became well known in the world tattoo community. This notoriety led to some much-needed paychecks. In an interview, Leppard explains his situation. "I would get an income from being the most tattooed man in the world, and would be photographed for the Guinness Book of Records, or featured on TV. . . . But it was a necessary evil to supplement my income support, or latterly my pension. It's not something I enjoyed."[26]

Paul Lawrence of Seattle, Washington, also chose to be tattooed for professional reasons. Working as a circus performer in the early 1990s, Lawrence was trying to figure out ways to improve his act—and one day inspiration struck. "I thought: I guess I could be a different color. That's a good idea. Or maybe even like a pattern. . . . If I had a jigsaw pattern, that would really be cool,"[27] he says in one interview.

Lawrence quickly acted on his idea. He had his entire body tattooed with interlocking puzzle pieces and adopted the stage name "The Enigma." The result was a glut of requests for personal appearances plus a big

Did You Know?

In 1995 The Enigma appeared on the TV show *The X-Files* playing a character called "Conundrum." This character was later made into an action figure.

25

bump in Lawrence's fan base. Still performing today, The Enigma proves that it is possible to turn body art into income.

Selling His Body

While The Enigma may earn money from his tattoos, he is not actually selling the skin off his back. One man, however, has done just that. Between 2006 and 2008 Switzerland resident Tim Steiner allowed Belgian

Tom Leppard (pictured) decided to tattoo his entire body with leopard spots. His goals of attracting attention and earning money from his body art have brought success in both areas.

artist Wim Delvoye to tattoo his entire back with an image of the Madonna surrounded by Asian and African ritual symbols. Working with an art gallery, Steiner and Delvoye then sold the tattoo to a German art collector. The sale price was €150,000 (euros), which is equal to about $200,000.

The contract regulating this sale has some interesting points. Steiner must exhibit his tattoo three times a year in public and private shows. After Steiner dies, the skin of his back will be stripped off, preserved, and given to the collector. The collector has the right to resell the work, either during or after Steiner's lifetime.

The tattoo on Steiner's back is doubtlessly a magnificent piece of work. The value of the transaction, though, lies more in the concept than the actual image. "It is a difficult work of art. It pushes the boundaries of the acceptable not only in relation to art, but also on a moral level and in that sense is quite scary," says Stephanie Schlieffer, a representative of the art gallery that brokered this macabre deal. "Tim had to question everything about himself, about his beliefs, what he thought about art. . . . It's not just a painting. It's a very fascinating and interesting journey."[28]

Indeed it is. And the art world is watching with interest to see how the journey will go. Steiner is a young man, so it may take decades for the answer to unfold. Only time will tell what life as a museum piece is really like.

Tattoos as Performance Art

An artist named Sandra Vita Ann Minchin has taken a uniquely personal approach to this question. Perhaps following in Steiner's footsteps, Minchin had her back tattooed in 2011, then sold the skin to a collector. Unlike Steiner, though, Minchin had most of her tattoo work done in sessions that were open to the public. The staged aspect transformed Minchin's tattoo from regular body art to performance art. As one reviewer explains, "Her work is intended to subvert the way in which we look at art. . . . She emphasizes the importance of seeing the resulting artwork not simply as a 'tattoo' but as a very considered piece of art."[29]

Did You Know?

In 2011 Tim Steiner spent four months on display at the Museum of Old and New Art in Tasmania, Australia. He perched on a stool for hours each day, letting visitors ogle his tattooed back.

Even more extreme is the work of renowned performance artist Mary Coble. Coble has conceived and been the centerpiece of several staged tattoo events. The most recent performance took place in 2008 and was entitled "Blood Script." Coble describes the event's concept in a recent article:

> I chose 75 . . . hateful terms and had them tattooed, without ink, onto the front portion of my body in a very ornate script. After each word was completed, watercolor paper was pressed against the fresh incision and a blood impression was created. As a hate speech amassed on my flesh, the wall beside me also filled with the hate speech.

> With this performance I set up a dichotomy between the "beautiful" visual of the text and the nasty meaning behind the words. Once the viewers were drawn in, they then considered how those words affected them personally.[30]

Coble's performance was a disturbing yet brave melding of ugliness and art. By submitting to the tattooist's needle, Coble felt physical pain that echoed the emotional pain of the words drilled into her flesh. She wanted the live audience to be moved by her discomfort. In this way Coble hoped to give her artistic message the greatest possible impact.

More Is Better

Most tattoo enthusiasts do not give as much thought to deep meanings as Coble does. In fact, some pay almost no attention to the symbolic aspects of tattoo. They just think tattoo art is beautiful. Many people think they will get just one small piece. They like the first one so much that they end up adding another—and another—and another. Before they know it, their skin is covered with permanent artwork.

The best living example of this compulsion may be Isobel Varley, an Englishwoman who holds the Guinness world record for being the world's most tattooed senior woman. Varley got her first small tattoo on a whim in 1986, when she was forty-nine years old. She loved the piece, and she immediately

Did You Know?

The marks made on Mary Coble's skin during her inkless tattoo performances disappeared within about six months.

A Circus Staple

Full-body tattoos became popular in America thanks mostly to the circus scene of the late 1800s and early 1900s. During this period every major circus kept at least one completely tattooed "freak" (as they were known) on staff.

At first these people worked mostly in sideshows. Tattooed men and women alike displayed their nearly naked bodies to crowds of amazed, gawking patrons. Some performers made up elaborate stories to explain their body art. A man named James O'Connell, for instance, claimed that he had been captured by savages and forcibly tattooed by a band of beautiful women. A woman who went by the stage name "La Belle Irene" said she had purposely tattooed herself as a protection against the unruly male "natives" of her Texas homeland.

The popularity of tattooed performers reached its peak in the late 1800s. By this time about three hundred people had turned themselves into living works of art in the hope of striking it rich on the circus circuit. This increased supply, however, dampened the novelty factor of full-body decoration. Tattooed performers turned to sword swallowing, fire eating, juggling, and other circus skills to beef up their acts.

Even these changes, however, failed to revive the public's flagging interest. As a result, tattooing faded away as a circus attraction. It survives today only in artwork and photos that commemorate this chapter in body art history.

asked the tattoo artist to do a second one. Shortly thereafter she went to another tattooist and got a few more pieces done.

Varley repeated this process multiple times. At some point she decided her tattoos were getting too scattered, and she solicited the help of yet another tattoo artist to unify her look. "He started to join them up. . . . We basically started at the top of my body and gradually worked our way down,"[31] Varley recalls.

Varley soon achieved a full body suit and then some. Today Varley is covered from her toes to the top of her skull with artwork. Only her face remains bare. Varley says she intends to leave it that way—but she is not positive. She says she might succumb to the temptation to fill her last patch of empty flesh at some point.

Some might consider Varley's behavior obsessive or even addictive. When asked if she is addicted to tattoos, Varley readily admits that she might be. "But it's more than that," she adds. "Once you

Isobel Varley, a native of England, holds the Guinness world record for being the world's most tattooed senior woman. She is covered with tattoos from head to toe in what is known as a full-body suit.

start something, it has to be finished, so things just seem to develop by themselves." Besides, she says, "I just get [tattoos] for their beauty. I love the way they look."[32]

Personality on Display

Many other tattoo enthusiasts feel the same way. They adore their ink. They feel that the images on their skin are works of art just as good as any that hang on museum walls—or perhaps even better. After all, says one scholar, "There is no art more personal than a tattoo. It's an expression that is not commissioned for a corporation or a museum or gallery, or for other, richer people. It's for you alone. It emanates from and conveys your deepest wishes, dreams, fantasies, fears, spiritual beliefs. . . . You are the inspiration for the image."[33]

The images in question, of course, are not just uniquely personal. Pounded deep into the skin, they are actually part of their owner's flesh and blood. It is hard to imagine how any art form, no matter how renowned, could be more intimate or more meaningful than that.

Did You Know?

Isobel Varley has spent more than five hundred hours under the tattoo needle to achieve her allover look.

Tattoo Artists

In a recent interview, an artist explains what his work means to him: "I have a belief that all artists are born artists. Oh, I know people can be trained and educated and then work in the arts, but there is more to art than wiggling a mouse. . . . That vision to see into other places, that insane burning desire to work through the night, that notion that if you don't work, you could lose your sanity . . . these aren't things that can be taught. They separate Artists with a capital 'A' from the rich kids going to art school."[34]

These ideas are not particularly fresh or new. It might surprise some people, however, to learn that they come not from a painter or sculptor but from a professional tattoo artist. Johnny "Thief" Di Donna worked in various fields of conventional art for fifteen years before picking up his first tattoo needle. Once he did, he never looked back. Now running his own tattoo studio in Savannah, Georgia, Johnny Thief is happier in his art than he has ever been before.

Why Tattoos?

Johnny Thief is just one of the many professionally trained artists who have entered the tattoo field in recent decades. This influx is due in part to the rising popularity of tattoos. As customer demand has risen, it has become more possible than ever before for tattooists to get plenty of work and earn a decent income. The explosion of tattoo shops has also created lots of job opportunities. Today a young artist may more easily find work as a tattooist than, say, as a graphic designer.

Easy opportunity, though, is seldom the issue for the tattoo world's most accomplished practitioners. Top tattooists actually prefer working on human skin above all other mediums. They consider themselves artists just as much as anyone whose work hangs in a museum. The only difference is that they practice their art on living canvases.

Different tattooists cite different reasons for their artistic interests. For Nes Andrion of Reno, Nevada, tattoo is partly a way of getting his work out into the world. "I wanted my art to be on a person, not on paper. . . . I wanted it walking around. When someone has a tattoo, they are displaying my work everywhere they go,"[35] he says. The permanent link between artist and client is part of what Andrion loves about his job.

Other tattooists do not care about permanency. They just like the fact that their work allows them to meet new people and hear new things every single day. Gerry Beckerman of Ava, Indiana, is part of this group. "I get such a wide variety of people," he responds when asked what he

A tattooist concentrates on her work at an international convention in Germany. The challenge of working on a living canvas appeals to many tattoo artists.

enjoys most about his work. "Some of them are more interesting than others, but all have a story . . . the path that led them to . . . getting a tattoo. Those stories are interesting to me."[36]

Still other tattooists cite the hard but fun task of working on living flesh. "It's a challenge moving and contorting [skin] to get into the right position to get the ink in the right way, let alone all the skin differentials you need to deal with. It is just one of the variables that make tattooing such an interesting and difficult media for artists to explore,"[37] explains a tattoo artist who calls herself Madame Lazonga. For Lazonga and others, achieving this goal is part of what makes tattooing more rewarding than conventional artwork could ever be.

Apprentice and Master

Young artists are well aware of these potential rewards. It is therefore not surprising that so many talented people are drawn to tattoo. Becoming proficient in this art, however, is a complicated process that requires years of practice. Only the most dedicated students will put in the time, effort, and cost necessary to master this tricky trade.

Nowhere is this truer than in Japan, where would-be tattooists serve grueling apprenticeships under master artists. The traditional training period is five years. Until recent decades, the apprentice lived with the master during this time and did household chores in return for sporadic tattoo education. As Japanese tattoo master Horihide vividly recalls, this education included years of observation. "If I had no work during the day, I would sit down on the left side of my master and watch his work from the distance. . . . I used to keep sitting straight for two hours and just watching my master's hands," Horihide says of his apprentice days. "The master would say to me, 'I'm not going to lecture you. You steal my techniques by watching me work.'"[38]

Today the Japanese apprenticeship model has changed a bit. Masters are not as exacting as they used to be, and most of them reportedly take a greater interest in their pupils. Aspiring tattooists are lucky that these changes have occurred, because there is no way around the apprenticeship requirement. The art of Japanese tattoo is complicated and

Did You Know?

Untrained, unskilled tattoo artists are known in the industry as "scratchers."

The Business Behind the Art

The business of tattoo involves much more than simply creating art on skin. Tattooists need to know about all sorts of non-art-related things to do their jobs properly, including:

Some basic anatomy. Tattoo artists must understand the skin's structure and function to produce a good tattoo. They also need at least a rough knowledge of the human nervous system to minimize the pain of their procedures and avoid possible nerve damage.

Blood-borne pathogens. Diseases such as hepatitis and HIV/AIDS spread through contact with infected blood. Tattoo is a bloody process, so artists must understand how to keep themselves and their customers safe.

Equipment operation. Wielding a tattoo machine and other equipment is much more complicated than swiping a paintbrush. Tattooists must master and maintain every piece of equipment to get the results they want.

Cleanliness. Tattoo artists are required by law to sterilize their equipment, keep their work spaces clean, and properly dispose of tattoo-related waste. They must know and follow the many rules that regulate these activities.

Paperwork. Most states require tattoo clients to sign consent forms before going under the needle. Contracts, invoices, and other types of paperwork are also part of the artist's daily routine.

Cardiopulmonary resuscitation (CPR). The tattoo process can be very uncomfortable and stressful for clients. Tattoo artists must know emergency medical techniques in case their human canvases faint or experience other difficulties.

steeped in obscure traditions and techniques. Anyone who wants to learn it must study long and hard under a master.

American artist Benny Her is a recent case in point. He became fascinated with tattoos when he met a Japanese master in the late 1990s. On a whim, Her moved to Japan and begged the master to take him on as an apprentice. He spent the next four and a half years learning to tattoo. The apprentice had no income during this period and was homeless for an entire year at one point. In the end, though, Her finally mastered his chosen trade and was allowed to accept customers.

Did You Know?

Japanese *tebori* is not in wide use today. Only an estimated five or six *tebori* masters still practice this art.

The road to this accomplishment was long and hard, but the now official Japanese tattooist has no regrets. "I think I was right to put all my chips on this," he says. "I'm not going to go be an insurance salesman or something."[39]

Keeping the Past Alive

Like Her, many modern-day tattoo artists are fascinated by old tattoo methods and designs. They feel these bits of the past are culturally important and deserve to be remembered, not to mention showcased. Tattooists around the world are therefore working to preserve the historical art of tattoo.

One aspect of this effort is the use of hand-tattooing techniques instead of modern machinery. Some Japanese tattoo artists, including one named Horimyo, are following this path. Horimyo works exclusively in a traditional style called *tebori*, which means "done by hand." In *tebori*, tattoos are poked dot by dot into the skin using handcrafted needles, brushes, and other implements.

The *tebori* process is hard and time-consuming, and it takes years to reach even basic proficiency. But Horimyo feels the results make the work worthwhile. "All handmade is the most valuable thing in any genre," he says. "When you look at sculptures, there is a big difference between machine-[made] ones and handmade ones. I think that applies to tattoo as well."[40]

Horimyo admits that machines do a better job on some types of tattoos, but he will leave that work to other artists. He thinks his role as a *tebori* master is more important. "It's an amazing technique, and we need to pass this on to the future. So I must continue, right?"[41] he says.

Tatau master Pili Mo'o is doing the same type of work in a different part of the world. Educated in classical Samoan designs and methods, Mo'o travels around the globe with a kit containing traditional tapping mallets, combs, and other implements. He fascinates audiences with live exhibitions of the Samoan tattoo skills developed over thousands of years. He will even tattoo audience members upon request.

Using a water brush, a traditional Japanese tattoo artist transfers the chosen design to the client's back. Once the special transfer paper is peeled away, the outlines of the design remain and provide a rough guide for the artist.

Being the Best

Being a top tattoo artist is hard work. A reality TV show called *Ink Master* shows exactly how hard by putting ten tattooists in the hot seat and subjecting them to weekly challenges. The contestants must produce their best work under crippling deadlines and conditions. Each week one tattooist is eliminated until only the best artist remains.

The competition is judged by heavily inked rocker Dave Navarro along with famed tattoo artists Oliver Peck and Chris Nuñez. The judges admit that the challenges can be very tough—but that, they say, is part of the plan. Professional tattooists must cope with many adverse conditions, and contestants should be able to do the same. In the end, the judges believe that good tattoo skills will always win out.

Two seasons into the show, this belief seems to be holding true. Rocky Rakovic of *Inked* magazine, for one, is glad. He explains his feelings in a recent article: "Stakes are . . . high. They are high for the contestants and high for the industry, as the eyes of the country will be, in essence, judging the claim that tattooing is an art. Until now, tattooing has only been a backdrop to shop drama and clients' stories, but *Ink Master* [puts] the focus on the craft and its process, rewarding those with stellar work, not just those with stellar looks or sparkling personalities."

Nuñez agrees with Rakovic's assessment. "A lot of complaints with tattoo shows are that they are not about tattooing anymore," he says. "Hopefully this is going to highlight the appreciation of tattoo art."

Rocky Rakovic, "Who Is the Ink Master?," *Inked*, December 6, 2011. www.inkedmag.com.

Getting onto Mo'o's to-tattoo list can be tricky. For one thing, the *tatau* master is booked far in advance. For another, Mo'o follows all traditional Samoan tattoo rules, one of which is not to tattoo after dark. "Be sure to book it before the sun goes down,"[42] advises a friend who schedules some of Mo'o's personal appearances.

Learning the Art of Modern Tattoo

While a few tattooists gravitate toward old methods, today many more artists prefer the new. Modern tattooing has its own equipment, techniques, and conventions. It is much easier to learn than traditional hand-executed styles, but that does not mean it is simple. Good tattoo artists spend years studying and learning before they are ready to create art on human flesh.

When starting this process, one recommendation has not changed from the old days. Aspiring tattoo artists are still strongly encouraged to seek apprenticeships with working tattooists. These positions are not easy to get. Experienced tattooists, especially the best ones, will not accept students who do not impress them. They want to see art portfolios to gauge an applicant's talent. They also need to be convinced that the would-be tattooist is serious about wanting a tattoo career. Young artists sometimes beg for months or even years before landing the apprenticeship they want.

Once this hurdle has been cleared, the aspiring artist will start to learn the basics of the tattoo trade. He or she will spend hours watching tattooists at work. The apprentice will also get familiar with the equipment, inks, and other supplies used on the job. In every spare moment the apprentice will draw, draw, draw, and draw some more to improve his or her tattoo design skills.

At some point the young tattooist will be deemed ready to wield an actual tattoo machine. This can be a scary moment—because usually the tattooist's first "client" is his or her own leg. Most professional tattooists can point out a number of poorly executed pieces on their thighs or calves that are permanent reminders of these practice sessions.

The self-tattooing process is sometimes painful, but it has many advantages. "It only costs me the materials used and I can stop when I want, not being on the clock. I can pick another time to layer any adjustments necessary and learn at the same time," says one typical artist-in-training. "Finding preferences [about equipment] on myself has been rewarding also."[43]

Did You Know?

A Japanese tattooist earns a new tattoo name after completing an apprenticeship. The name always starts with the letters *Hori*, which come from a word meaning "to carve."

Creating the Art

Actually applying tattoos is only one part of a tattooist's job. Tattooists who consider themselves fine artists would say it is not even the main part. The most important aspect of their work, these people believe, is designing the piece of art that will be etched into the client's skin.

The design phase is a multistep process that begins with a consultation. The client sits with the tattoo artist and describes the tattoo he or she wants in as much detail as possible. Sometimes clients have just a vague vision. At other times they know exactly what they want, right down to the last detail. Either way, an open exchange of ideas is the key to success. "The clearer our communication is about your ideas, the clearer I can visualize it and produce it for you,"[44] explains one tattooist.

Once the consultation has occurred the client leaves, and the tattooist gets to work. He or she may spend days leafing through art sources, sketching, and manipulating image software to create the requested image. Line weights, colors, perspective, light angles, and many other factors are tweaked until the artist thinks everything is perfect.

At this point the client returns and views the artwork. He or she makes sure everything has been done exactly as envisioned. If not, the client asks for changes. The artist alters the image as many times as necessary to get it right.

When the client finally approves the finished piece, the artist copies the work's outlines onto a piece of special transfer paper. The paper is stuck onto the client's skin. When it is peeled away, the outlines remain as a rough guide for the artist. The client checks and approves the image's size and position. Only then can the tattoo application finally begin.

Masters of the Trade

Some tattoo artists excel at design but are not particularly gifted at the physical tattooing process. Others are just adequate as artists, but they are wizards when it comes to wielding tattoo equipment and applying work to skin. A very few lucky tattooists are geniuses in both areas—and when these talents meet, worldwide recognition is sometimes the result.

There is no universal agreement about which tattoo artists are "the best." Certain names, however, tend to come up over and over. One often-mentioned icon of the trade is Guy Aitchison, an American tattooist who is known for the incredible detail and texture of his work. Aitchison, who has written a series of technique books known informally as "the tattooer's Bible," emphasizes the importance of pursuing one's art outside the tattoo arena. "[It] is critical for all artists who have any interest in exploring what they are capable of to occasionally do so without the normal restrictions of the tattooist-client relationship," he says. "I can't emphasize enough how much a second medium can contribute to our artistic success as tattooists."[45]

While Aitchison has made his name through technical virtuosity, tattooist Paul Booth has made his by scaring people. Booth specializes in demented artwork featuring demons, skulls, gore, lost souls, and other dark topics. Despite his themes, Booth calls himself laid-back. "I think it's because I get all the aggression out in my art,"[46] he laughs in one interview.

When the laughter stops, though, Booth reveals a serious artistic streak. "Tattooing is really just another medium for an artist, whether you are sculpting, painting, or tattooing. All should have the same level of artistic ability,"[47] he says. To further this notion, Booth organized an exhibition called the ArtFusion Experiment in 2001. This event gathered artists of all mediums, including tattoo, to create collective, spontaneous works of art. Still occurring today, ArtFusion events have helped to bring tattoo art and the artists who create it into the public eye.

Celebrity Tattoo Artists

Reality TV shows that feature tattoo shops and professionals have done the same thing, but to an even greater degree. The tattoos-on-TV trend started in 2005 with a show called *Miami Ink*. Airing on The Learning Channel (TLC), *Miami Ink* showcased the daily doings of a Miami, Florida, tattoo shop. The shop was run by an attractive and heavily tattooed artist named Ami James, who was recruited for his TV-friendly looks and personality. "I [am] a people person. . . . I'm outspoken and, to some, a little obnoxious, and apparently that's what [the producer] was looking for,"[48] James recalls in one interview.

Did You Know?

Tattoo apprenticeships can be expensive. Most apprentices pay for the privilege of learning from an experienced tattooist.

James signed up for *Miami Ink* because he liked the idea of giving viewers an insider's glimpse of the tattoo industry. He expected his professional life to be more or less business as usual. He did not expect what actually happened: James became a reality TV celebrity. He was recog-

Headstrong, talented, and heavily-inked tattoo artist Kat Von D (pictured in 2010) gained fame on the television show Miami Ink. *She and other celebrity tattoo artists have tried to show tattooing in a positive light.*

nized everywhere he went, even by people who had no previous interest in tattoos. Like it or not, James had become the public face of the tattoo industry.

James's employees earned their share of attention, too. The viewing public especially loved a heavily inked female tattooist named Kat Von D. Young, attractive, headstrong, and blazingly talented, Von D seemed to be a made-for-TV dream character. In interviews the artist revealed her artistic motivations. "I never wanted to be on TV, but . . . if I didn't take this opportunity, someone else would. For me, the thought of a medio-cre female tattooer representing everything I love . . . did not sit well with me. This was my opportunity to show tattooing in a positive light, and give it all I have,"[49] she explains.

Von D, James, and other celebrity tattoo artists have worked hard toward this goal. Their efforts, how-ever, have not always been appreciated by the tattoo community. Many professional tattooists dislike tattoo shows and feel that they present an unrealistic view of the industry.

James agrees with this criticism to a point, but he also defends his work. "The show was going to happen. It was inevitable," he says. "And I think one thing that most people agreed on in the tattoo industry—whether they hated us or not—was that it was good for business. . . . It showed everybody that tattoo shops weren't all filled with bikers who butcher people. Tattoo artists are just artists . . . trying to make a living."[50]

And it can be a very satisfying living. For artists with true talent, tat-too offers rewards that start with a paycheck but go far, far beyond.

Did You Know?

After leaving *Miami Ink* in 2006, celebrity tattooist Kat Von D went on to star in her own tattoo reality series, *LA Ink*. Von D's show aired from 2007 to 2011.

Tattoo Art on Display

The art of tattoo has gone through many ups and downs in its long history. At some times and in some places tattoos have been held in the highest esteem. In other eras and areas inked skin has suffered from a bad reputation. It has been linked in the public mind with criminal behavior, bad taste, poor social status, and other undesirable qualities.

Today tattoos are on the upswing. Body art is losing its bad connotations and becoming increasingly popular. More than that, it is also emerging as an art form worthy of critical recognition. In recent decades many venues, including some of the world's most prestigious ones, have chosen to exhibit and celebrate the artistic side of tattoos.

Breaking Museum Ground

Historians point to a 1995 show as the first significant exhibition of this type. The show in question was presented by the Drawing Center, a well-known art institution in New York's SoHo district, and it was titled *Pierced Hearts and True Love: A Century of Drawing for Tattoos*. This showing of Western tattoo flash and its Asian influence, explains one critic, "marked the first major New York City tattoo exhibition under the distinguished heading of art. When displayed within a gallery context, the meanings and functions of the objects were recognized as having aesthetic value."[51]

Pierced Hearts included three hundred drawings of tattoo art from the 1800s to the present. Well thought out and assembled, the exhibition was an eye-opener for many artists and critics. It was also a commercial success—so much so that the show eventually went on a national tour. It visited Miami's Museum of Contemporary Art and many other institutions, spreading its tattoo-positive message wherever it went.

Other organizations noticed the success of *Pierced Hearts*. They saw a trend in the making, and they soon followed the Drawing Center's lead by launching their own tattoo exhibitions. In 1999 New York's South Street

---

The American Museum of Natural History exhibit Body Art: Marks of Identity *presented a wide range of tattooing, piercing, and other body art traditions. A display from the New York exhibit appears here.*

Seaport Museum celebrated an influential US tattooist in a display titled *American Tattoo: The Art of Gus Wagner*. Meanwhile, across town, the American Museum of Natural History opened its doors on a show titled *Body Art: Marks of Identity*. These shows had different focuses, but their effects were the same: They both pushed the art of tattoo a little further into the public limelight. One tattoo historian says that *Body Art* in particular was "a major breakthrough for the museum to show its outstanding collection and to create a context where that work could be understood."[52]

Yet another museum attempted a similar feat a short time later. In 2002 the Royal Museums of Greenwich, England, hosted a six-month show titled *Skin Deep*. The exhibition brought together objects that showed the development and diversity of tattoo art over the previous two hundred years. It included displays showcasing tattoo art's uses in the modern world.

Did You Know?

Gus Wagner may have been the first American tattooist to perform cosmetic tattooing of women's lips, cheeks, and eyebrows. He pioneered this technique in the early to mid-1900s.

The Show Goes On

Skin Deep and other early exhibitions were important because they tried to change the way the art world saw tattoos. They succeeded surprisingly well. A decade after the first tattoo display, most art aficionados were willing to admit that tattoos might have some artistic merit.

The first decade of exhibitions may have swayed critics but the second decade truly won them over as museums around the world paid increasing attention to tattoo art. They developed shows that focused on specific cultures, techniques, and areas of interest. With each show the art of tattoo moved a little further into the art world's mainstream consciousness.

A 2009 Chicago exhibition called *Freaks & Flash* is one example of this trend. Spanning the late nineteenth century to the 1970s, this show presented examples of flash. In tattoo lingo, *flash* refers to predesigned tattoo images that customers can pick off a wall or out of a catalog. Considered boring by most tattoo enthusiasts today, flash once represented the cutting edge of tattoo design. The exhibit celebrates the artists who created these images and paved the way for modern tattoo art.

A 2011 exhibit called *The Art of the Sailor* looked at a different aspect of tattoo. Hosted by the Columbia River Maritime Museum in Astoria, Oregon, this display examined modern tattoo's roots in the traditions of long-ago sailors. It presented the first European explorers' role

The Painted Prince

Centuries ago, a heavily tattooed slave named Giolo was displayed as a living work of art. Known as the "Painted Prince," Giolo was native to the Philippine island of Mindanao. He was purchased in 1690 by an English explorer named William Dampier. In a later account of his voyages, Dampier recalls Giolo's remarkable markings:

He was painted all down the breast, between his shoulders behind; on his thighs (mostly) before; and in the form of several broad rings or bracelets round his arms and legs. I cannot liken the drawings to any figure of animals or the like; but they were very curious, full of great variety of lines, flourishes, chequered work, etc., keeping a very graceful proportion and appearing very artificial, even to wonder, especially that upon and between his shoulder-blades.

Dampier brought his human canvas to England. Obliged to do his master's bidding, the unfortunate Giolo spent the next year parading himself before a curious stream of London's elite. The display was hugely popular—but it took a heavy toll on the health of the main attraction. Tired and malnourished, Giolo became ill with smallpox. He died soon afterward, forever ending history's first tattoo exhibition.

William Dampier, *A New Voyage Round the World*. London: Adam and Charles Black, 1937. http://gutenberg.net.au.

in bringing tattoo to the western world, then traced the art of tattoo from this early origin to its present-day status. "The thing we want people to remember from visiting this exhibit is that the current interest in tattoos and tattoo designs has its roots in strong maritime traditions that really kicked off in the 18th century,"[53] says the show's curator. By displaying these traditions, *The Art of the Sailor* gave people yet another glimpse into the tattoo world.

So did *Tattoo Honolulu*, an exhibition that ran from 2012 to 2013 at the Museum of Art in Honolulu, Hawaii. Featuring historical photographs, modern tattoo works, and ten visiting skin artists, this event sought to commemorate and celebrate the fine art of traditional Hawaiian tattoo. "Most artists believe that the basis of great art is drawing, and tattoo artists in Hawaii are incredible draftsmen," boasts museum director Stephan Jost. "They use this skill to create extraordinary tattoos."[54] These tattoos include bold black-inked patterns as well as artwork depicting lizards, ferns, and other traditional Hawaiian images. By displaying this work, Jost hopes to preserve a fascinating part of Hawaii's artistic history.

Did You Know?

A famous tattooist named Sailor Jerry created much of the nautical-themed flash still seen today. His work was very popular in the mid-1900s.

On Permanent Display

Exhibitions can be fascinating, but they are also temporary. They only run for limited periods. For a more lasting look at the art of tattoo, enthusiasts can visit dedicated tattoo museums around the world. Open to the public, these facilities display private collections that have been lovingly gathered piece by piece and decade by decade by their tattoo-loving owners.

The premier collection of this type is found in the Netherlands. Founded by Dutch tattoo artist Henk "Hanky Panky" Schiffmacher, the Amsterdam Tattoo Museum shows off more than sixty thousand tattoo-related items. Objects on display range from historical artifacts to old equipment and swaths of preserved human skin. The museum also displays artwork and prints from the world's most famous tattooists, both past and present. "There's really nothing else quite like it. Nothing that covers such a broad range of tattooing history, from the tribal world through contemporary tattooing," says Lars Krutak, an anthropologist from the Smithsonian National Museum of Natural History. "I see it as an incredible place to learn about the meaning of tattooing from all angles, from all time periods."[55]

The Amsterdam Tattoo Museum may be the world's biggest permanent tattoo display, but it is not the only one. Some avid collectors have created their own smaller exhibits for the public to enjoy. A typical example is the Lucky Supply Tattoo Museum in Largo, Florida. Showing tattoo art and memorabilia dating back to the early 1900s, this collection is owner Jimmy Whitlock's way of giving back to the profession he loves. "Tattooing has come a long way over the decades," he explains on the museum's website. "It was the pioneers of the art, who practiced in secret

Lucky Supply Tattoo Museum in Florida boasts tattoo art and memorabilia dating to the early 1900s. Among the artifacts on display is this tattoo kit from the 1930s.

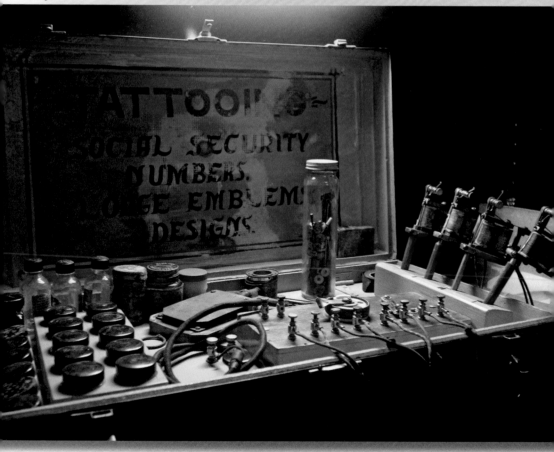

Permanent Souvenirs

As tattoos become increasingly respected and popular, a phenomenon called tattoo tourism is on the rise. Tattoo tourists are people who actively seek out the tattoo culture of the places they visit. Some do this simply to learn about the culture's traditions and techniques. Others have a more permanent goal in mind. They want some ink of their own to commemorate their foreign adventures.

A traveler named Jazmine Atienza offers an extreme example of this practice. When Atienza traveled to the Philippines in 2011, she says, "I was already into tattoos. . . . I had designed Filipino tattoos in my head." Atienza learned about a ninety-five-year-old tattoo artist living on a remote Philippine mountaintop and decided to pay the woman a visit.

A harrowing twelve-hour trek through a typhoon followed. The final leg of the journey involved a dangerous hike through muddy ravines. Atienza did eventually reach her destination, however, where she received the reward she sought: an authentic Filipino tattoo hand-tapped into her skin in the traditional manner.

Atienza loves her tattoo. Even more, though, she loves the story behind the ink. "For me it ended up being very much about the journey," says this tattoo tourist. "It's not just about the mark as much as it is about the experience. It goes beyond being a novelty experience to being a really meaningful one."

Quoted in Dana McMahan, "Tattourism: Permanent Souvenirs Make Their Mark," NBC News, January 29, 2013. www.nbcnews.com.

and were looked down upon in the eyes of the public, who allowed this art and industry to grow into what it is today. . . . In my own small way I am trying to preserve the beauty and history of the art of tattooing for future generations."[56]

Whitlock is not alone in this effort. Many tattoo enthusiasts around the world maintain similar displays. These displays are often connected to tattoo shops. Visitors can enjoy a slice of tattoo history, then pop into the studio to get a little artistic ink of their own.

Group Gatherings

While tattoo museums preserve the past, gatherings called tattoo conventions celebrate the present in a loud, crowded, and sometimes outrageous way. These events bring together dozens or even hundreds of professional tattooists from all over the world. Each tattooist has a separate booth where he or she can display art samples and do tattoos. Convention attendees can watch the artists at work or, if they are brave enough, make appointments to go under the needle themselves.

Tattoo conventions serve many artistic purposes. For attendees, they offer a way to meet renowned tattooists and get the tattoo of their dreams. They also let people see tattoo art in action while connecting with fellow enthusiasts and enjoying music, food, drinks, contests, and other fun events.

Participating tattoo artists reap many benefits from tattoo conventions, too. They have the chance to expose their art to new audiences. They get to enter tattoo contests with categories such as "Best Skull," "Most Unusual," "Best Arm Sleeve," and "Best of Show." But most important, they get to see what other top artists in the field are doing. It is an inspiring and artistically supportive atmosphere that makes people feel good about their chosen profession. "I thought to myself just how great it was to be working at a show with so many talented artists and mingling with them in the off hours,"[57] said one tattooist after attending a recent convention.

With all these positives, it is no surprise that tattoo conventions have become immensely popular around the world. The biggest conventions are usually organized as traveling shows. The three-hundred-artist Ink America Tour, for example, was scheduled to visit eight cities across America in 2013. So was the Ink Life Tour, which featured over two hundred top tattoo artists. High-energy and high-quality, these shows and others like them attract massive crowds wherever they go.

Did You Know?

Henk "Hanky Panky" Schiffmacher has tattooed many rock artists, including the late Kurt Cobain of Nirvana and members of the Red Hot Chili Peppers and Pearl Jam.

Tattoos Online

Not everyone appreciates this type of scene. Some people would rather see and appreciate tattoo art from the privacy of their own homes. For these people, online displays may be the answer. Websites devoted to every imaginable aspect of tattoo art are open twenty-four hours a day, seven days a week to the viewing public.

Some of these sites take a historical approach. One example is Vanishing Tattoo's Tattoo Museum, an online collection that starts with tribal body art and works its way up to the present. The site offers full indexes of tattoo designs and symbols plus extensive catalogs of celebrity body art along with tattoo photos, videos, facts, links, and more. It is a good starting point for anyone interested in perusing the basics of the tattoo world.

Other tattoo sites display no work or products of their own. They simply provide gathering places where the public can create the exhibit. An example is Check Out My Ink, a social media site where members post pictures of their tattoos. Boasting nearly 150,000 members and four hundred thousand tattoo photos in early 2013, this site proves that when it comes to tattoo art, human canvases are desperate to be part of the show.

Covering the Industry

Tattoo enthusiasts like to keep up with developments in the tattoo world, too. To meet this need, publishing companies have launched many tattoo-oriented magazines in recent decades. These magazines approach the tattoo scene from different angles. Some focus on tattoo culture and news. Others pay more attention to tattoo artists, artwork, or other aspects of the tattoo world. With so much variety, today's newsstands hold something for every tattoo enthusiast.

A lifestyle magazine is the most popular of the tattoo offerings. With a circulation of over 140,000, *Inked* covers all aspects of the tattoo culture, including music, fashion, art, sports, and more. It features in-depth profiles of tattooists, tattooed celebrities and personalities, shops, events, and other topics related to the tattoo world. Sometimes called "the out-

Did You Know?

Tattoo convention attendees can sometimes volunteer to be human canvases for tattoo competitions. Canvases cannot pick their own art, but they are tattooed free of charge.

siders' insider magazine," *Inked* speaks to interested readers with or without tattoos.

Skin & Ink is another widely read magazine. This publication reaches about one hundred thousand people per month. Its goal is to publicize the fine art aspect of the tattoo industry through full-color photographs, inspiring stories, and profiles of top tattoo artists and shops. A bit more targeted to the industry than *Inked*, this magazine appeals to people who enjoy tattoos more for their artistic value than their wilder side.

For even more art focus, readers can turn to the twin publications *Flash* and *Tattoo*. *Flash* is mostly pictorial and is meant to showcase the

Tattoo conventions, which take place around the world, provide venues for those who appreciate the art of tattoo. One participant at a London tattoo convention shows off her fanciful foot art.

tattoo world's most striking art without a lot of text support. *Tattoo* features much of the same art shown in *Flash*, but it supplements the images with in-depth articles about the work's creation and creators.

Flash and *Tattoo* are not as widely read as the lifestyle magazines. They appeal to the true art enthusiasts of the tattoo crowd. One happy subscriber explains why he likes *Tattoo* in particular. "Why get tattoos without knowing about advancements in tattooing, or the awesome people that do it? People who have tattoos should really enjoy the articles and the people that keep tattooing alive," he says. "Respect those that make a living sharing their art with the world."[58]

Read the Book

The ultimate respect, of course, is the desire to actually own someone's work—or beautiful photographs of it, anyway. People who feel this way can find books that showcase the fine art of tattoo. There are many to choose from. One online bookstore lists more than one thousand titles under the heading of "Tattoo Art and Photography."

Books about tattoo art take different angles on their topic. The compendium or catalog is one common format. This type of book assembles artwork from a variety of tattooists in one colorful array. A recent example is *Tattoo Prodigies: A Collection of the Best Tattoos by the World's Best Tattoo Artists*. Compiled by famed tattooist Mike DeVries, this large-format volume is packed with photos of tattoos along with their creators' more traditional artwork. The collection graphically demonstrates that the world's best tattooists are not limited to skin alone. They can produce impressive artwork in many different media.

Fans of one particular tattoo artist may want to delve a bit deeper into his or her life and work than a compendium will allow. For these readers, books that showcase specific tattooists may be helpful. The many books on Japanese artist Horiyoshi III are good examples of this format. Horiyoshi's followers can choose among works such as *36 Ghosts, 100 Demons, 108 Heroes of the Suikoden*, and *Dragons*. As their titles suggest, these books gather the *tebori* master's best work on specific topics. The volumes are

Did You Know?

About three-quarters of all tattoo magazine readers are male.

expensive and hard to find, but they are considered classics by tattooists and historians alike.

Not quite as classic, but perhaps more useful, are volumes that present collections of tattoo images, or flash. Books of this type may be handy research tools for readers who are considering getting inked. Perhaps more important, they serve as reference books for working or would-be tattooists. "For someone who wants to learn how to draw tattoos and learn the traditional tattoo style of drawing, I would say it's pretty handy to have,"[59] says one reader in regard to *Tattoo Bible*, a high-quality collection of five hundred tattoo images.

This volume and many others are more than just fun reads. They are portals into the ever expanding world of tattoo. By presenting tattoos in a format long associated with fine art, books give tattoos a sheen of respectability. They also make them accessible to anyone, anywhere, anytime. Today no one needs to enter a studio to see tattoo art on display.

The Art of Body Piercing

Like tattoo, body piercing is a technique used to modify the human body. This practice has existed in cultures all around the world for thousands of years. During this time, body piercing has had many meanings. It has been used for religious reasons, for identification, for spiritual protection, and much more.

Body piercing is not valued only for its deeper meanings. Many people simply like the way it looks. Some people like it so much that they suffer through multiple piercings for the sheer pleasure of beautifying themselves. In these cases, piercing can be seen as an art form. Increasingly accepted in modern times, body piercing today has become a popular type of private, public, and even performance-based art.

Body Piercing Basics

In its most basic sense, the term "body piercing" refers to any deliberate puncturing of the human skin or body. The goal is usually to create a hole in or through which jewelry can be worn. The jewelry choices are often highly visible or even outrageous. "I originally got piercings to wear spiky jewelry as I loved it! . . . I think my earrings are much cooler than standard ones,"[60] says one person with multiple piercings.

Modern piercing is done mostly with sterile needles of different shapes and thicknesses. The piercer marks the body part to be pierced, then carefully pushes the needle through the flesh. The jewelry follows the needle through the hole. Some piercing needles have hollow ends that hold the jewelry and pull it through the puncture wound as it is made.

For larger piercings, tools called dermal punches may be used. Punches are used to remove circular chunks of tissue. They are commonly used on the upper ear and other areas with thick cartilage. Punches are not legal in some parts of the United States, so piercers in these areas must resort to needles for every piercing, no matter how big or difficult.

The art of body piercing has a long and colorful history. In some of the world's cultures, lip piercing and the stretching of the lip to allow for specially crafted jewelry is a sign of beauty. An Ethiopian villager displays this type of piercing.

Piercing seems like a simple procedure, but there is more to it than meets the eye. Professional body piercers undergo extensive training that may include seminars, online training courses, and apprenticeships. They need a host of knowledge about the equipment and techniques used in the piercing process. Piercers, like tattooists, must also understand a large number of related topics, including human anatomy, microbiology, sterile technique, CPR, and many more. The best piercers are experts in all of these subjects, not just masters of the piercing arts.

Although practically any body part can be pierced, some piercing sites are more popular today than others. Earlobes are by far the most common piercing site. Noses, eyebrows, lips, and navels are other frequently pierced sites. Among more adventurous groups, nipple and genital piercings offer a very personal source of artistic expression.

Traditional Piercing

All of these types of piercing have been practiced not only in modern times but in the recent and distant past as well. Many cultures of many eras have practiced piercing as a distinct art form.

This was true in ancient Egypt, where ears were pierced and earrings were worn to enhance female beauty. The most typical jewelry was a dangling golden hoop, although other styles undoubtedly existed. Navel piercing was also practiced by the Egyptians, although historians believe pierced navels were not nearly as common as pierced ears. Evidence suggests that this type of adornment was reserved for Egyptian royalty and other high-ranking individuals.

In the area that is now Alaska, lip piercing was once considered the height of fashion. Some of the area's native men and women wore one or two ivory plugs called labrets in their lips. The initial piercing was small, but wearers widened it over time by inserting bigger and bigger labrets. Over time the lip stretched until, says one writer, "[it] hung down, exposing teeth and gums. . . . Larger labrets sometimes

Did You Know?

Old-time sailors pierced their ears as a type of funeral insurance. They hoped the jewelry would pay for a proper burial if their bodies washed up on distant shores.

Eyeball Jewelry

They say beauty is in the eye of the beholder. One extreme piercing trend turns this statement into the literal truth! Gerrit Melles, a corneal surgeon at the Netherlands Institute for Innovative Ocular Surgery, has developed a way to implant jewelry directly into the human eyeball. Called JewelEye, the implants are made of flat metal and shaped like hearts, half moons, and a few other simple objects. Once placed, JewelEye products remain permanently in the eye for the world to see.

An article describes the JewelEye implantation procedure and result: "An ophthalmologist anesthetizes your eye, then makes a microscopic incision in the conjunctiva, the eye's transparent outer membrane. The doctor drops a tiny piece of jewelry . . . into the incision, and the procedure is over. It takes 10 minutes and costs about $4,000, and you spend the next week feeling as if you have a piece of sand in your eye. When the conjunctiva heals, you can't feel it (even when you rub your eyes)."

Eye piercing sounds downright dangerous. But Melles claims that the risk of infection is actually lower than it is with other piercings, since the jewelry is enclosed in the eye and never exposed to germs. Time has also shown that JewelEye implants do not move within the eye, even after years of blinking and rubbing. Still, this extreme trend has never undergone official safety testing, and it is not regulated by government agencies. For now, it is a bit too daring for all but the most extreme piercing enthusiasts.

Rebecca Skloot, "Eyeball Jewelry," *New York Times Magazine*, December 12, 2004. www.nytimes.com.

interfered with speaking and eating and had to be removed."[61] The jewelry was immediately reinserted when these activities were complete to restore the beauty of the wearer's pierced mouth.

Less troublesome but equally treasured were the pierced noses of various cultures. Nasal jewelry historically has been worn on both sides of the nose and through the septum (the wall of skin, cartilage, and bone that separates the nostrils). Many Tlingit of southeast Alaska sported nose rings in the septum. Side nose piercings were preferred in long-ago India and Pakistan, where facial jewelry communicated a woman's marital status. And nose piercings of many types were sported by the Aztecs, the Mayans, and the tribes of New Guinea. These people used bones, feathers, and other piercing adornments to broadcast their strength, status, and general attractiveness.

Today, many people continue to enjoy the piercing traditions handed down through the centuries. They adopt traditional styles because they like their meanings or their look. By choosing these styles, modern piercing enthusiasts help to keep the past alive.

Piercing Royalty

This approach does not suit everyone. When it comes to piercing, many people have no interest in history or traditions. They see piercing as a way to express their individuality and creativity, and they seek new and ever more outrageous ways to flaunt their passion. Over time they may amass a collection that crosses the line from being mere jewelry to becoming a work of art.

Rolf Buchholz of Germany is a living example of this approach. Buchholz got his first piercing when he was forty years old, and he became an immediate fan of the practice. He soon pierced his lips, his eyebrows, his nose, his ears, and his genitals. He made sure the piercings were arranged in regular patterns so they would be aesthetically pleasing. Today Buchholz sports a beardlike forest of metal studs and rings that frame his mouth, along with twenty-five bars threaded across the eyebrows and multiple strategically placed nose piercings. With a total of 453 studs and rings from head to toe, Buchholz holds the Guinness world record as the world's most pierced man.

Buchholz's excesses have made him a well-known figure in the piercing world. Even so, Buchholz does not begin to approach the piercing status of the world's most extensively decorated person. Elaine Davidson, a native of Brazil who now lives in Scotland, sported nearly seven thousand piercings at last count in 2011. The number has undoubtedly gone up since then because Davidson has no intention of quitting her hobby anytime soon. "I am going to have more piercing done all over my body . . . I'm enjoying [it],"[62] she says in one interview.

The enjoyment is evident by the sheer quantity of the result. Davidson's entire face, including her forehead, cheeks, tongue, and chin, is covered with metal jewelry. She has bars running through the skin of her arms, her legs, and most other body parts. She does not publicly display her genital piercings but proudly says she has a lot of them, about 150 of which are internal.

Davidson does not have any deep motivation for turning herself into a living jewelry display. She just likes it. "I want to change myself, and I think it's fun," she explains. "I'm very proud of what I am wearing and what I'm doing. Some people look at me and think it's a mask, [but] I don't mind what they think. . . . I love it."[63]

Did You Know?

Some Eskimo labrets were carved to look like tusks. A man wearing two of these adornments, one through each side of the mouth, looked a lot like a walrus.

Public Piercing

While Davidson collects piercings just for fun, others do it specifically to attract attention. They pierce their own skin or allow others to do it in public while onlookers gasp in disgust. These open displays of pain can be considered a type of performance art, where piercing is as much about the process as the end result.

Piercing enthusiasts Chris Elliot and Staysha Randall know all about this type of display. Between 2010 and 2011 the pair vied to win the world record for most body piercings in a single sitting. Elliot got the contest going in May 2010, when he publicly endured 3,100 consecutive needles poked through his skin. Randall upped the ante with 3,200 needles in June 2011. Not to be outdone, Elliot submitted to the needle once again in August 2011, this time braving 3,900 piercings in seven hours and forty-six minutes. All of these feats were filmed and submitted to the *Guinness Book of World Records* as well as various public websites.

With their piercing performances, both Elliot and Staysha had an end goal in mind: a world record. Other people who endure public piercings, however, have no such aspirations. They simply like the reaction they get from doing something unusual and shocking. They dream up all kinds of piercing stunts to get the attention they crave.

In 2008 acupuncturist Wei Sheng of China managed to attract world press coverage with his unique piercing activities. Sheng was trying to

Elaine Davidson, the world's most pierced woman, is a living jewelry display. As of 2011, she had nearly seven thousand piercings over her entire body.

think of an original way to celebrate the upcoming Olympic Games—and one day it came to him. "We are used to seeing people paint national flags on their faces in other Olympic Games, so I thought why not just put the flags in vertically?"[64] he recalls. Sheng followed through by mounting small flags representing more than two hundred nations on acupuncture needles and plunging them into his scalp. He topped off the presentation with a needle shaped like an Olympic torch, which he slid under the skin of his forehead.

Apparently emboldened by his own feat, Sheng soon kicked things up a notch. Documented by the press, Sheng inserted 2,008 needles into his head and cheeks. The needles were tipped with small crosses colored red, blue, yellow, green, and black—the five colors of the Olympic games. It was a display of pride, patriotism, and pain the likes of which most people had never seen before.

Theater of Pain

Sheng's piercings may have been eye-catching to the uninitiated. For true piercing fans, though, this type of display would barely raise an eyebrow. The piercing world supports a thriving underground performance art scene that features some of the most shocking skin-puncturing acts imaginable. Serious performers go to even more extremes—much more extreme than simply sticking a few pins into their heads.

The practice of suspension is one of these extremes. In suspension, metal fish hooks are driven through various parts of the performer's flesh. There may be just one hook or many, depending on what the performer intends to do. When the hooks are in place, ropes are attached to them and the performer is lifted completely off the ground. He or she will hang there, dripping blood, anywhere from a few seconds to hours or even days.

Most suspension performers say the practice is a spiritual experience. By letting an audience watch, they hope to share a little bit of the mystic joy they are feeling. "I don't really do it to entertain the people," says Alex Vasquez, a frequent suspension artist. "For me, personally, it's just a way of reaching a higher state of existence, an out-of-body experience. . . . It's more about ritualistic rites of passage."[65]

Not all artists take such a cerebral approach. Some admit freely that they enjoy piercing themselves before audiences at least partly because of the shock value. A sideshow performer who goes by the stage name

> ## Did You Know?
> Rolf Buchholz's facial piercings are so heavy that they pull his lower lip downward. His bottom teeth are always a little bit exposed.

Running the Gauntlet

Today's piercing fans can browse catalogs full of navel barbells, nipple shields, tongue rings, and other types of body jewelry. Made of the highest quality materials, these adornments raise body decoration to an art form.

This bounty of choices arose from the work of Jim Ward, a piercer and jewelry designer sometimes called "the granddaddy of the modern piercing movement." In 1975 Ward opened America's first piercing-only studio, Gauntlet, in West Hollywood, California. He soon realized that there was very little body jewelry on the market. "Piercing enthusiasts were making do with earrings and all kinds of improvised contrivances," Ward recalls in a 2004 article.

To solve this problem, Ward started designing his own wares. He developed many simple styles that are industry standards today, including the beaded ring and the barbell. He also introduced more artistic pieces. Nipple shields, for example, were designed to surround and draw attention to pierced nipples, just as picture frames enhance artwork.

Ward's designs were not only popular among Gauntlet's clients, they also revolutionized the piercing industry. "It's been almost 30 years since I started Gauntlet, but the ideas and innovations that it pioneered are very much with us today," Ward says.

Jim Ward, "Gauntlet's Jewelry Design Legacy," Gauntlet Enterprises, May 28, 2004. www.gauntletenterprises.com.

Lucifire numbers herself among this group. "I'm a bit of an adrenaline junkie. I'm not afraid of blood and I love its symbolism," she says of her work. "I love making shows, especially shows that affect people deeply and strongly. There's no better praise than a few fainters or vomiters, which means that the combination of reality overload and theatrical elaboration has done its job."[66]

Considering what Lucifire does on stage, it is not surprising that she sometimes elicits this type of reaction. Lucifire has been known to slice her skin open and to drive long nails into her head. Perhaps most alarming, she sometimes drills holes into her arms, inserts wax candles, and then sets the candles aflame. Pierced and proud, this human candelabra leaves a trail of melted wax and spilled blood as she struts across the stage.

Outrageous Piercings

While performers like Lucifire get extreme piercings for audiences, others do it simply for their personal pleasure. They like the way their bodies look with various holes and adornments that nature never intended. By modifying their flesh, these people express their individuality and creativity in ways that seem outrageous to some viewers but artistic to others.

An individual who calls himself Mr. Tetanus exemplifies this approach. Nearly twenty years ago Mr. Tetanus pierced his ankle with a metal spike nearly half an inch thick. The spike passes between the Achilles tendon and the bones of the lower leg. If removed, it leaves an open hole big enough to stick a finger through. Today Mr. Tetanus is recognized worldwide as a radical work of human art.

A man known as Pauly Unstoppable enjoys an even more notorious reputation in the piercing community. Unstoppable has modified his body in too many ways to list, but piercings are an important part of the package. Unstoppable is especially well known for the enormous holes in both sides of his nose. An inch and a half wide, the preposterous piercings are big enough to accommodate huge plugs, sharp knives, scissors, or a variety of other objects that Unstoppable favors as jewelry.

Unstoppable and others who sport extreme piercings are considered attention-seekers by some. Unstoppable emphasizes, though, that his motivation is entirely personal. "When I didn't have modifications, I felt alien in a world of humans. Through modification, through adorning myself and filling in the blanks, I'm making myself more human. I'm changing my body because I want it to look perfect,"[67] he says.

But is it art? Unstoppable thinks so—and to him, that is the only opinion that matters. "Some people will go, 'You've gone too far, you've wrecked your life,

Did You Know?

To achieve the world record for most piercings in a single sitting, Chris Elliot had to endure an average of more than eight piercings per minute for close to eight hours.

Suspension is an extreme form of body piercing performance art. Sterilized hooks (shown) are driven through the flesh and then participants are suspended from a ceiling or other structure.

you've wrecked your face,' but if you don't know me and you haven't talked to me, then you have no right to say that, because all you're doing is judging me based on your personal biases," he says. "When I see myself, I'm content with what I've done. What I see is perfect."[68]

Everyday Art

Most piercing fans would not go as far as Unstoppable has in the quest to beautify themselves. The basic feeling Unstoppable expresses, however, is common in the piercing world. In an online forum, one young woman explains her thoughts. "I have a few piercings. I got them because I like the way they look on my body, and I can always take them out if I decide to get something else or they are inappropriate for work,"[69] she says.

For other people, piercing is not just about looks and convenience. They seek a deeper artistic meaning in their body adornment. As one person with thirteen piercings explains, "It's a way of personalizing myself. Something that I have and control that no one can take from me. Something that in some way, shape, or form can set me apart from everyone else."[70]

This statement may cut to the heart of piercing's appeal. In today's crowded, anonymous world, people are desperate to demonstrate that they are special or different in some way. Piercing is so personal that is almost like a signature on the skin. For this reason, piercing is an extreme but exceptional way of expressing one's personality. It is no wonder that people use this practice to turn themselves into living works of art.

Did You Know?

A man named Fakir Mustafar is known as the father of the modern primitive movement, which is built around the art and practice of suspension.

Introduction: Are Tattoos and Body Piercings Art?

1. Nicolas Michaud, "Are Tattoos Art?," in *Tattoos—Philosophy for Everyone: I Ink, Therefore I Am*, ed. Robert Arp and Fritz Allhoff. Malden, MA: Wiley-Blackwell, 2012, p. 29.

2. Michaud, "Are Tattoos Art?," p. 29.

3. Austin Prey, "POINT: Tattoos," *Dartmouth*, April 24, 2009. www.thedartmouth.com.

4. Michaud, "Are Tattoos Art?," p. 33.

5. Michaud, "Are Tattoos Art?," p. 37.

Chapter One: The Traditional Art of Tattoo

6. William Dampier, *Dampier's Voyages*. London: E. Grant Richards, 1906, p. 539.

7. Samuel Wallis, quoted in "History of Polynesian Tattoo," Tahiti Tatou, 2008. www.tahititatou.com.

8. James Cook, *Captain Cook's Journal During His First Voyage Round the World*, 1768–71, ed. Captain W.J.L. Wharton. London: Elliot Stock, 1893. www.gutenberg.org.

9. Joseph Banks, *The Endeavour Journal of Sir Joseph Banks*, 1768–1771, March 31, 1770. www.gutenberg.org.

10. Banks, *The Endeavour Journal of Sir Joseph Banks*, 1768–1771.

11. Quoted in Lars Krutak, "Embodied Symbols of the South Seas: Eastern Oceania," Lars Krutak—Tattoo Anthropologist, 2010. www.larskrutak.com.

12. Krutak, "Embodied Symbols of the South Seas: Eastern Oceania."

13. Quoted in Krutak, "Embodied Symbols of the South Seas: Eastern Oceania."

14. Quoted in Major-General Robley, *Moko; or Maori Tattooing*. London: Chapman and Hall, 1896. http://nzetc.victoria.ac.nz.

15. Karl Groning, *Body Decoration: A World Survey of Body Art*. New York: Vendome, 1998, p. 222.

16. Quoted in Jon Patrick, "Ancient Art of the Japanese Tebori Tattoo Masters/Ink in Harmony," The Selvedge Yard, April 20, 2010. www.theselvedgeyard.wordpress.com.

17. Groning, *Body Decoration*, p. 195.

Chapter Two: Living Works of Art

18. Mary Lynn Price, "Excerpts from an Interview with Mary Lynn Price," Skin Stories: Tattoo Stories, PBS, 2003. www.pbs.org.

19. Price, "Excerpts from an Interview with Mary Lynn Price."

20. Anonymous, "How to Get a Full Body Tattoo," eHow. www.ehow.com.

21. Quoted in Sofia Mella, "Lucky Diamond Rich: My First Bodysuit," *Tattooed Heart*, October 14, 2010. http://thetattooedheart.net.

22. Quoted in Mella, "Lucky Diamond Rich: My First Bodysuit."

23. Quoted in Lukas Zpira, "Interview Lucky Diamond Rich," Hacking the Future, February 6, 2009. hackingthefuture.blogspot.com.

24. Quoted in Jack Ruby Murray, "Zombie Boy," *Bizarre*, June 2008. www.bizarremag.com.

25. Quoted in Alessandra Codinha, "Interview with Rich Genest, the Zombie Boy," *Women's Wear Daily* Online, June 18, 2012. www.wwd.com.

26. Quoted in Neil Stephen, "The Cat Who Came In from the Cold," *Guardian*, October 27, 2008. www.guardian.co.uk.

27. Quoted in Steve Gilbert, ed., "Enigma Interview," based on interviews at the Houston Tattoo Convention (January 18, 1996) and at Northern Ink Xposure, Toronto (June 21, 1999), Tattoos.com Ezine. www.tattoos.com.

28. Quoted in Jessica Dacey, "Swiss Takes Love of Tattoos to the Extreme," Swissinfo, September 26, 2008. www.swissinfo.ch.

29. Simon Brouder, "'Skin and All' Art Sale," *Kerryman*, July 13, 2011. www.kerryman.ie.

30. Quoted in *New Gay*, "Interviews: Artist Profile: Mary Coble," April 15, 2008. thenewgay.net.

31. Quoted in Ashley, "Tattooed Granny," *Bizarre*, February 2008. www.bizarremag.com.

32. Quoted in Ashley, "Tattooed Granny."

33. Ellen Shapiro, "Skin Deep," *Print*, January/February 2004, p. 98.

Chapter Three: Tattoo Artists

34. Quoted in Shannon Larratt, "Johnny Thief Tattoo Interview in BME/News," *BME/News Modblog*, February 29, 2008. news.bme.com.

35. Quoted in Dan Wetzel, "Tattoo Artist Living His Dream with the Help of Colin Kaepernick as His Canvas," Yahoo! Sports, January 25, 2013. sports.yahoo.com.

36. Quoted in Karen L. Hudson, "Interview with Tattoo Artist, 'Ink-slinger,'" About.com: Tattoos/Body Piercing. tattoo.about.com.

37. Madame Lazonga, "Everyone's Skin Is Different," Tattoo Road Trip, December 14, 2011, tattooroadtrip.com.

38. Quoted in Patrick, "Ancient Art of the Japanese Tebori Tattoo Masters/Ink in Harmony."

39. Quoted in Brian Ashcraft, "The Hardcore World of Japanese Tattoos Will Make You Stronger," Kotaku, March 2, 2012. kotaku.com.

40. Horimyo, interview by Tokyo Fashion News, Tokyo Fashion, July 19, 2012. tokyofashion.com.

41. Horimyo, interview by Tokyo Fashion News.

42. Quoted in Ken Smith, "Sacred Ink," *Chico (CA) News & Review*, October 4, 2012. www.newsreview.com.

43. Colin James, "Tattooing Yourself," June 15, 2009. knink.com.

44. Alycia Harr, "My Design Process," Sacred Temple Tattoos, October 4, 2010. www.alyciaharr.com.

45. Quoted in Crash, "Guy Aitchison: Heavyweight Tattoo Champ," *Prick, n.d.* www.prickmag.net.

46. Quoted in Chuck B., "Paul Booth Brings Dark Things to Life," *Prick*, December 2003. www.prickmag.net.

47. Quoted in Chuck B., "Paul Booth Brings Dark Things to Life."

48. Quoted in Stan Haraczek, "Interview with Ami James from *Miami Ink*," *Inked*. www.inkedmag.com.

49. Kat Von D., "Get to Know Kat," TLC *Miami Ink*. tlc.howstuff works.com.

50. Quoted in Haraczek, "Interview with Ami James from *Miami Ink*."

Chapter Four: Tattoo Art on Display

51. Vanishing Tattoo, "Tattoos in the USA," February 4, 2013. www.van ishingtattoo.com.

52. Quoted in Vanishing Tattoo, "Tattoos in the USA."

53. Quoted in Lori Tobias, "Tattoo Exhibit in Astoria, 'The Art of the Sailor,' Recalls Origins, Significance of Skin Drawings," *Oregonian*, April 24, 2011. blog.oregonlive.com.

54. Quoted in Honolulu Museum of Art, "Tattoo Honolulu Exhibition Overview," February 4, 2013. honolulumuseum.org.

55. Quoted in Ivan Quintanilla, "Tattoos, Through Time: A New Museum for Amsterdam," *New York Times*, January 10, 2012. intransit .blogs.nytimes.com.

56. Jimmy Whitlock, "About Us," Lucky Supply Tattoo Museum. www .lstattoomuseum.com.

57. Aaron Bell, "Aaron Bell Visits the Milan Convention," *Skin & Ink*, October 2005. www.skinink.com.

58. bigjaytanner, "Excellent Depiction of Tattoo Culture," Amazon.com review, November 30, 2002. www.amazon.com.

59. Jcoops, "Not a Bad Start," Amazon.com customer review, August 15, 2010. www.amazon.com.

Chapter Five: The Art of Body Piercing

60. watermelon, "Why Do You Have Piercings?," Body Jewellery Shop: Forum, September 22, 2011. www.bodyjewelleryshop.com.

61. University of Pennsylvania Museum of Archaeology and Anthropology, "Piercing Ancient and Modern." http://penn.museum.

62. Elaine Davidson, "World's Most Pierced Woman," video clip, Diagonal View, YouTube, July 16, 2008. www.youtube.com.

63. Davidson, "World's Most Pierced Woman."

64. Quoted in Emma Graham-Harrison, "Human Pincushion Welcomes Olympics with Head of Flags," Reuters, July 10, 2008. www.reuters.com.

65. Quoted in Jennifer Squires, "Surreal Suspensions," *Ashland (OR) Daily Tidings*, June 21, 2005. www.dailytidings.com.

66. Quoted in Danielle Clark, "Lucifire: Queen of 'Grotesque Burlesque,'" *BMEZINE* ModBlog, August 20, 2003. news.bme.com.

67. Quoted in James Doorne, "Body-Mod King," *Bizarre*, April 2008. www.bizarremag.com.

68. Quoted in Doorne, "Body-Mod King."

69. Abbie, "Why Did You Get a Tattoo or Piercings?," follow-up reply, Yahoo! Answers, April 2, 2012. answers.yahoo.com.

70. deepsoul, "Why Did You Get a Tattoo or Piercings?," follow-up reply, Yahoo! Answers, April 2, 2012. answers.yahoo.com.

Books

Elayne Angel, *The Piercing Bible: The Definitive Guide to Safe Body Piercing*. Berkeley, CA: Celestial Arts, 2009.

Cypi, *Oriental Tattoo Art: Contemporary Chinese and Japanese Tattoo Masters*. Berkeley, CA: Gingko, 2013.

Mike DeVries, *Tattoo Prodigies: A Collection of the Best Tattoos by the World's Best Tattoo Artists*. Northridge, CA: Memento, 2010.

Doralba Picerno, *Tattoos: Ancient Traditions, Secret Symbols and Modern Trends*. Edison, NJ: Chartwell, 2012.

Dale Rio, *Planet Ink: The Art and Studios of the World's Top Tattoo Artists*. Minneapolis: Voyageur, 2012.

Superior Tattoo, *Tattoo Bible: Book One*. Stillwater, MN: Wolfgang, 2009.

Kat Von D, *High Voltage Tattoo*. New York: Collins Design, 2009.

Kat Von D, *The Tattoo Chronicles*. New York: Collins Design, 2010.

Jo Waterhouse, *Art by Tattooists: Beyond Flash*. London: Laurence King, 2009.

Websites

Check Out My Ink (www.checkoutmyink.com). This social media site allows users to share pictures of their favorite tattoos.

Discovery Fit & Health (health.howstuffworks.com). This site includes an excellent in-depth reference guide that explains how tattoos work, along with their health risks and other related topics.

Guide to Body Piercings (tattoo.about.com). This site is a good overview on the subject of body piercing. It includes descriptions of popular piercings plus information about procedures, safety, and more.

Skin Stories: The Art and Culture of Polynesian Tattoo (www.pbs.org/skinstories). Supporting a PBS documentary, this site is an anthology of stories, images, and history gathered from the hot spots of Pacific tattoo.

The Tattoo Museum (www.vanishingtattoo.com). This site offers a wealth of information on tattoo history, design, symbolism, culture, and much more.

Tattoo Road Trip (tattooroadtrip.com). This site offers a wealth of articles on every imaginable aspect of tattooing.

Picture Credits

Cover: © Markus Cuff/Corbis, Thinkstock Images

Marc Alex/AFP/Newscom: 30

AP Images: 45

© Bettmann/Corbis: 37

© Damaske, Jim/Zuma Press/Corbis: 49

© Felipe Dana/AP/Corbis: 23

© Simon Ford/Loop Images/Corbis: 62

© Werner Forman/Corbis: 15

© Rick Friedman/Corbis: 5

© Chris Gordon/Corbis: 42

© Bob Krist/Corbis: 9

© Tony Melville/Reuters/Corbis: 53

Mike Moore/Mirrorpix/Newscom: 26

© Yuriko Nakao/Reuters/Corbis: 18

© Robin Utrecht Fotografie/HillCreek Pictures/Corbis: 57

© Lance Rosenfield/Corbis: 66

© Boris Roessler/epa/Corbis: 33

Kris Hirschmann has written more than two hundred books for children. She owns and runs a business that provides a variety of writing and editorial services. She lives near Orlando, Florida, with her husband, Michael, and her daughters, Nikki and Erika.

391.65 H669   CAR
Hirschmann, Kris,
Tattoos, body piercings, and art /

CARNEGIE
04/15

Friends of
Houston Public Library